BOOK ANALYSIS

Written by Isabelle Consiglio
Translated by Ciaran Traynor

Have Mercy on Us All

BY FRED VARGAS

Bright
≡Summaries.com

FRED VARGAS

FRENCH NOVELIST AND ESSAYIST

- **Born in 1957 in Paris.**
- **Notable works:**
  - *This Night's Foul Work* (2006), detective novel
  - *An Uncertain Place* (2008), detective novel
  - *The Ghost Riders of Ordebec* (2011), detective novel

Fred Vargas (real name Frédérique Audoin-Rouzeau) was born in Paris in 1957. She is a writer, historian and archaeologist who has worked as a medieval archaeologist at Belgium's National Fund for Scientific Research. Her pseudonym comes from the diminutive (Fred) of her given name and the character Maria Vargas, played by Ava Gardner in the film *The Barefoot Contessa* (directed by Joseph L. Mankiewicz in 1954). The author's twin sister, the painter Jo Vargas, chose the same pseudonym.

Fred Vargas has currently published around 15

detective novels, as well as some philosophical essays. Her novels have been extremely successful and have almost all won prizes either in France or abroad. Fred Vargas is currently one of France's most famous detective writers.

HAVE MERCY ON US ALL

A DETECTIVE NOVEL WITH A HINT OF NOIR FICTION

- **Genre**: detective novel
- **Reference edition**: Vargas, F. (2004) *Have Mercy on Us All*. Trans. Bellos, D. London: Vintage.
- **1st edition**: 2001
- **Themes**: plague, murder, vengeance, investigation, panic

Have Mercy on Us All was published in 2002 and is Vargas's ninth novel. The title of the book in French, *Pars vite et reviens tard* ("leave quickly and come back late"), refers to the advice given by medical guides in the Middle Ages that flight is the best response to a plague epidemic. The plot combines an investigation in modern-day Paris with a description of different plague epidemics, which a serial killer is using to frighten the city. We can assume that the author drew on her knowledge as a medievalist to write this novel. *Have Mercy on Us All* won the Prix des libraires and the Grand prix des lectrices de Elle in 2002.

SUMMARY

THE ANNOUNCEMENT OF THE PLAGUE

Joss Le Guern is a former Breton sailor. After he is shipwrecked, he attacks the owner of his ship and almost kills him, which leads to him being sent to prison for two years. After he gets out, he moves to Paris. This is where his great-great-grandfather appears to him during a heavy night of drinking and suggests that he take up the family job as town crier. Town criers used to deliver the news and announcements made by the inhabitants of remote villages.

Joss therefore decides to do just that and sets up a box in Paris where the inhabitants can put announcements and notes about how they are feeling. He cries out the news three times a day on a square somewhere in Paris. However, for the past three weeks he has been receiving strange messages written in Old French and Latin which announce the return of a terrible plague. He decides to go to see an old friend, Decambrais, a former prisoner nicknamed "the scholar" who identifies the messages as extracts from manuscripts describing different plague epidemics. The two decide to warn the police and go to see Adamsberg.

During this time, the Commissaire Jean-Baptiste Adamsberg has been transferred to the Paris murder squad. A young mother has come to lodge a complaint about the strange inscriptions on the doors of her building: an upside-down '4' written in black ink. After consulting a medievalist, the commissaire discovers that the number is actually a cross written in one stroke and is supposed to ward the plague away from the houses it is written on. These curious symbols begin to appear in flats across Paris. Adamsberg establishes a link between Joss's mysterious messages and the symbols which are spreading across the city. His curiosity leads him to go to listen to Joss's announcements to get a better idea of what these strange messages might mean.

Joss leaves his squalid one-bedroom flat to live with Decambrais, where he meets the other tenants: Damascus, who has a skate shop; Lizbeth, a former prostitute from America and something of a diva; Eva, who has just run away from her violent husband; and Marie-Belle, Damascus's unassuming sister.

THE FIRST LEADS

The narrator takes the reader to a see a woman called Narnie, whose son-in-law Arnaud is visiting her. He is apparently the one who is tracing the signs on the doors. The old woman is raising rats, which she believes are carrying the plague, and is sending Arnaud with letters filled with fleas to future victims. She is convinced that her family has magic powers, since her parents survived a plague epidemic.

Joss's messages for the day announce the first victims of the plague. A body is discovered in a block of flats in Paris and an envelope full of fleas is found near the body. The paper is identical to the kind used for the missives that the town crier has been receiving. Adamsberg and his assistant Danglard launch an investigation. They learn that the victim did not die of the plague, but was bitten by fleas and then strangled. Two other victims are found shortly afterwards. The people of Paris begin to panic: they trace the number four on their doors to protect themselves from the plague. Adamsberg is convinced that the killer is among the crowd that comes to hear Joss's news every morning.

The press gets wind of the rumour and reminds the residents of Paris about the plague epidemic which hit the city in 1920. Adamsberg asks a psychiatrist for help in order to draw up the killer's psychological profile. He thinks that culprit is personally linked to the plague. The commissaire does some research on the 1920 epidemic. He is also intrigued by Marie-Belle's other brother, who she takes care of because he seems to be psychologically fragile.

A new victim is discovered in Marseille and Adamsberg goes to investigate. As he continues his investigation, he discovers that the rich are now wearing diamonds on their left ring finger to protect themselves from the epidemic. The commissaire remembers that he saw a flash from someone's hand during Joss's crying. When he gets back to Paris, he takes Damascus in for questioning and sees that the man is indeed wearing a diamond on his left hand. He therefore becomes the main suspect. Moreover, he has fleas on him and has direct access to Joss's box. Adamsberg also discovers that he does not have a clean criminal record: he was wrongly accused of having thrown his girlfriend out of a window.

A stranger then comes to the police station claiming that his life is in danger: he has found a flea-filled envelope under his door. Adamsberg guesses that he has a mysterious past. Under pressure, the young man eventually admits that he was part of a band of seven gangsters who tortured a man and raped his girlfriend.

THE CONCLUSION

Adamsberg establishes a link with the past of Damascus, who had perfected a device for manufacturing honeycomb steel alloys which made them far less likely to fail. A major company boss then kidnapped him to steal his patent. After she was raped, his girlfriend committed suicide and Damascus was accused of murder. With the help of his grandmother, he prepared his revenge in prison using the family myth about the plague. His aim was to eliminate the gangsters who had attacked him and his girlfriend. Narnie is arrested and admits to everything, as she is convinced that the victims truly did die of the plague. Her family survived a plague epidemic in Clichy in 1920. There are still three of Damascus's torturers to be killed.

The commissaire is convinced that a third person has been entrusted with eliminating the remaining targets. Damascus and his grandmother still do not know that the fleas were actually not carrying the plague. After chasing an individual coming out of Marie-Belle's house, Adamsberg discovers that Damascus's father has led a double life: he recognised his first son, but not his other two children from another marriage: Marie-Belle and her brother Antoine. It is these two illegitimate children who followed Damascus to strangle the victims – they are the culprits. They wanted to get Damascus jailed for murder and steal his sizeable inheritance.

The real culprit, Marie-Belle, is not prosecuted because she has fled, leaving her confession for Adamsberg. Since they are not guilty of the murders, Damascus and his grandmother are let off. The commissaire decides not to tell the old woman that her grandson's torturers were not actually killed by the plague.

CHARACTER STUDY

JOSS LE GUERN

A former sailor who is very proud of his Breton origins, Joss Le Guern is sent to prison after violently attacking the owner of his ship. An aggressive alcoholic with no real family ties, he washes up in Paris and does a few odd jobs before embracing his family profession of town crier. His great-great-grandfather, Nicolas Le Guern, born in 1832, appears to him from time to time to offer advice.

Joss had a difficult childhood: he was sent to a boarding school at an early age, where he was beaten. He therefore distrusts strangers. He is used to being alone, and expresses himself in a direct, crude manner, mostly with a sailor's vocabulary: "The spherical vesicles of that kind of seaweed were called floaters, and Joss reckoned the word suited Adamsberg's eye to a T. The commissaire's floaters were buried beneath a protective overhang of untidy, bushy brows" (p. 88). Joss remains impassive: he does not fear the strange warnings that he reads and does not believe that the plague has returned to Paris for a second.

DAMASCUS VIGUIER (ARNAUD HELLER-DEVILLE)

Damascus is a secondary character at the start of the book and only becomes important in the second half of the story. He owns a skate shop called Rolaride and lets Joss work at the back. Damascus does not care very much about his appearance: his long hair is often dirty and he never really wears much clothing, even in winter.

The reader only learns about his painful past later on: his father was violent, but he was a brilliant student and perfected a chemical procedure to make metals more solid. After being captured and tortured by a company boss who wanted to steal his patent, Damascus's life was turned upside-down: he was accused of murdering his girlfriend, who actually committed suicide. As he was raised with the family legend of being able to sow the plague and survive, he works out a plan for revenge with his grandmother. He is a fragile, mentally broken character. Although he trusts Marie-Belle, his half-sister who he came across by chance, she eventually disappoints him as much as his discovery that the family power is a lie.

COMMISSAIRE JEAN-BAPTISTE ADAMSBERG

Born in the Pyrenees and transferred to the Paris murder squad, Adamsberg is a little brown-haired man with an unkempt appearance. He is a dreamer who has no real method to the way he goes about his investigations: he trusts his instincts, which generally lead him to the solution, and he is wary of using new technology. However, he is very sensitive to human drama: he easily detects the psychology of suspects or his colleagues.

A solitary character, the commissaire goes for long walks every day to reflect on the case that he is currently working on. He has been seeing Camille for several years, but he cannot express his feelings to her. She finds him in bed with another woman, an action that he later regrets without being able to apologise for it.

ADRIEN DANGLARD

Unlike his superior, the commissaire's assistant Danglard is the definition of a logical character. He values scientific proof and employs rigorous investigative methods.

Danglard is not much to look at physically, but he is still a touching character. Few of his collea-gues know that his wife left him and their five children. He has never recovered and drowns his sorrows alone at night with beer. He takes in Camille after Adamsberg cheats on her.

DECAMBRAIS (HERVÉ DUCOUEDIC)

A distrustful, discreet man, Decambrais is a former history teacher from Brittany who was wrongly accused of assaulting a student. He is a very well-read man (he is nicknamed "the scholar") who makes lace in his free time, which results in no end of mockery from his neighbours. Moreover, Decambrais is the first person who works out the killer's messages. He rents out rooms in his house to people in distress.

LIZBETH

Lizbeth is one of Decambrais' tenants. She is a former American prostitute and cooks for the whole household. She has a warm character with a brilliant smile and works as a jazz singer every night in a cabaret. She does not trust men and has no illusions about love.

ANALYSIS

FRED VARGAS AND NOIR FICTION

Noir fiction is often associated with the detective genre, of which it is a subgenre. It became popular in the United States between the First and Second World Wars. Noir fiction overturns the elements of the classic detective novel, namely:

- the identification of an infallible upholder of the law, namely the detective;
- the resolution of the investigation by the arrest of a suspect who is clearly guilty;
- characters with little psychological depth;
- a very stereotyped plot.

Noir fiction's main objective is to describe a particular social reality to identify the origin of the crime. The investigations generally take place in the outskirts of big cities or in the heart of poor areas. They are led by a commissaire or detective who often uses illegal methods, such as violence or bribes, to get to the bottom of the mystery. The wrongdoer is not always punished, since the gang networks often escape justice.

Noir fiction is a modern type of literature, and *Have Mercy on Us All* clearly fits with this genre. The novel describes the violence of the poor neighbourhoods of Paris and the instability of their inhabitants. Finally, the case is not really closed since the real culprit, Marie-Belle, manages to escape the law.

A DESCRIPTION OF THE MODERN WORLD

Vargas's book describes the daily life of a number of characters in a city that is far from the clichés normally found in works about Paris.

The characters all have a secret life or a painful past:

- Adamsberg cannot express his feelings or have a fulfilling romantic relationship;
- Danglard's wife left him to raise their five children alone;
- Joss Le Guern was sent to a boarding school and was subjected to violence when he was a child;

- Damascus went through hell: he was tortured, his girlfriend killed herself and he was sent to prison;
- Decambrais was accused of a crime he did not commit;
- Lizbeth has prostituted herself and lived on the streets.

None of the characters in this book seem to lead a simple, happy life. On the contrary, they are all psychologically complex. Society has mistreated them and many of them have fashioned themselves a second identity to protect themselves. Duality is a constant theme in Vargas's works: she already tackled it in *The Three Evangelists*.

These characters also tend to live in poor, violent areas. Their daily lives are dark and worrying:

- Joss has to survive on odd jobs;
- Narnie lives in a squalid house in Clichy;
- the majority of the characters seek refuge in bistros;
- the corridors in their apartment buildings are unsafe places;
- the street lamps along the canal do not work;
- Damascus is beaten up violently.

Society also seems to include a number of contradictions and injustices: "Damascus did five years' prison for a crime that never happened. Today he's been released for crimes he only thought he committed. Marie-Belle is on the run for carnage that she ordered. Antoine will be sentenced for murders he didn't choose." (p. 318)

The description of the modern world as Vargas sees it is dark, but also touching, since the majority of the characters try to get out of the mess they are in. The writer therefore does not present a completely pessimistic image of reality, as is often the case in noir fiction.

COLLOQUIAL, INVENTIVE LANGUAGE

The author describes Parisian life with the help of colloquial language. The tone of the conversations is often direct and coarse: "You have to have really lost it to spend your time spouting rubbish in a public place. Should get himself properly laid, that guy, that would clear his head a bit." (p. 122)

The plot unfolds at the pace of Joss Le Guern's

announcements, which set the pace of the novel and break with the general tone of the narrative. The presence of this intertext in Old French introduces a second level to the plot, since the characters have to investigate the origin of these messages. The documents concerning the plague epidemics of the plague introduce a historical element into the novel. *Have Mercy on Us All* is also filled with clues: Vargas drops hints about the killer's identity throughout the book, as we see when Marie-Belle's second brother is mentioned and when the protagonists visit Narnie. Finally, the different extracts of the texts concerning the plague can also be viewed as part of a code.

FURTHER REFLECTION

SOME QUESTIONS TO THINK ABOUT...

- Fred Vargas is a specialist in the Middle Ages. Does her passion come across in *Have Mercy on Us All*? Justify your answer.
- Contrast the two inspectors in the novel, Adamsberg and Adrien Danglard. Do they go about their investigations in the same way as other great detectives such as Columbo or Sherlock Holmes?
- What makes *Have Mercy on Us All* an example of noir fiction?
- In what way does *Have Mercy on Us All* differ from classic detective novels?
- Duality is a constant theme in Vargas's work. Explain how with the help of examples from the book.
- Is the novel optimistic or pessimistic? Give a detailed answer.
- Are the protagonists of *Have Mercy on Us All* heroes? Justify your point of view.

- What is the function of Joss Le Guern's announcements?
- In your opinion, is the cinema adaptation of the novel faithful to Vargas's work? Does it convey the atmosphere? Justify your opinion.
- In your view, why was this novel so successful?

We want to hear from you!
Leave a comment on your online library
and share your favourite books on social media!

FURTHER READING

REFERENCE EDITION

- Vargas, F. (2004) *Have Mercy on Us All*. Trans. Bellos, D. London: Vintage.

ADAPTATION

- *Have Mercy on Us All*. (2007) [Film]. Régis Wargnier. Dir. France: Gaumont Film Company.

Bright ≣Summaries.com

More guides to rediscover your love of literature

www.brightsummaries.com

Although the editor makes every effort to
verify the accuracy of the information published,
BrightSummaries.com accepts no responsibility for
the content of this book.

www.brightsummaries.com

Ebook EAN: 9782808000703

Paperback EAN: 9782808000710

Legal Deposit: D/2017/12603/463

Cover: © Primento

Digital conception by Primento, the digital partner of
publishers